Success Stories 101

A practical tool for interview preparation.

8 Steps for creating interesting, credible and memorable stories about your professional achievements.

Frank Rolles, MBA & Jennifer Rolles

DEDICATION

To our children: Reach your true potential, remain humble, but do not hide your light under a bushel basket. Share your talents and success stories with the world and give thanks for your gifts each day.

Contents

Introduction

This book is intentionally short. It is meant to be a practical and hands-on guide which you can go through in about an hour. During that time, we will guide you through the process of creating a success story from one of your professional achievements. Once you've learned the process, you can repeat it with additional stories. Each new story can be structured in about 30 minutes.

Your success stories can be used in a number of venues. The aim of this book is to help you learn to develop credible, interesting, and memorable stories you can share in an interview, performance review, or networking situation.

As humans, we prefer our communication in story format. There is research that shows it; but, just think about it for yourself. When we read a book, watch a movie, or hear a story, we relate to the characters involved. We feel for them and can imagine being in their shoes.

We experience the situation vicariously and learn from stories almost as well as we learn from personal experience. We have been programmed for thousands of years to share and learn using stories - from cave drawings to modern cinema.

In business communication we are taught to be more formal, crisp, and factual. We have been told to get to the point as quickly as possible, develop an elevator pitch, and provide quick responses to questions.

In our continuously evolving high-tech world, communication forms and forums continue to spawn: texting, Twitter, etc. It seems that the trend in communication is moving even further toward short and quick.

So why bother with story? Because unlike plain facts and figures, bulleted lists, and emotionally void presentations, we need rich human story to make what we are communicating resonate and stick in the minds of our audience.

This book was born from an in-person workshop that we created to help people develop success stories to share in interviews and on the web. We have delivered our live workshop to audiences of MBA students and other groups of professionals since 2010.

The process of developing success stories is simple but the results are powerful. Participants in our workshops comment that attending the course and going through our 8-step process has changed the way they think about their work experience. They say the class boosts their confidence and prepares them to respond more effectively in interviews.

Here is what a few people have said about our workshop:

"As a financial person I missed the boat on how to effectively tell my story. This class provided the tools to change that from this point forward." -Scott Todd, workshop participant

"I'd been telling my students that their STAR stories were too long, but now I realize that the real problem was that they were too boring." - Mike Schaefer, Assistant Director, Career Management Center, Kellogg School of Management

"If you know WHAT to do--PARs, COARs, SOARs, STARs, and/or FABs, but don't feel you know HOW, you should attend the Rolles' seminar. It's the best 'how-to' on developing and telling your 'success' stories that I've heard. Frank knows his material inside and out, as reflected in the bibliography he shares with participants, and he doesn't hold anything back. He gives you a step-by-step guided tour of the art and science of talking about your accomplishments. Don't miss this opportunity to learn from an expert." - Eugenia Kaneshige, Managing Partner, Norwood Career Advisors

Our goal in this book is to provide guidance and tips on how to improve the way you communicate your talents and accomplishments so they will stand out and be remembered.

By purchasing this book you also have access to our Success Stories 101 web application (www.successstories101.com) and training for no additional charge. The web application includes video training and space to develop and store your success stories online. You will also be able to print additional 8-step worksheets if you prefer to work on paper.

The book and online information are essentially the same; so, it doesn't matter which method you prefer to use. See the Success Stories 101 Online section at the back of this book for instructions on how to sign in to the web application.

Whether you decide to use the book or the web application, let's get started!

Destination and Path

First, we will talk briefly about what factors help people commit new information to memory because we ultimately want our audience to remember our stories.

Next, we will discuss why communicating via stories is more effective than other forms of communication such as lists, charts, or short response approaches. This is not to say other forms of communication are not useful or appropriate for certain situations; but, wrapping information with story is more impactful.

Finally, we will walk through our 8-step process for creating interesting, credible, and memorable stories you can share in an interview or online. This is meant to be a hands-on workshop; so, we hope you will develop one of your own success stories along the way.

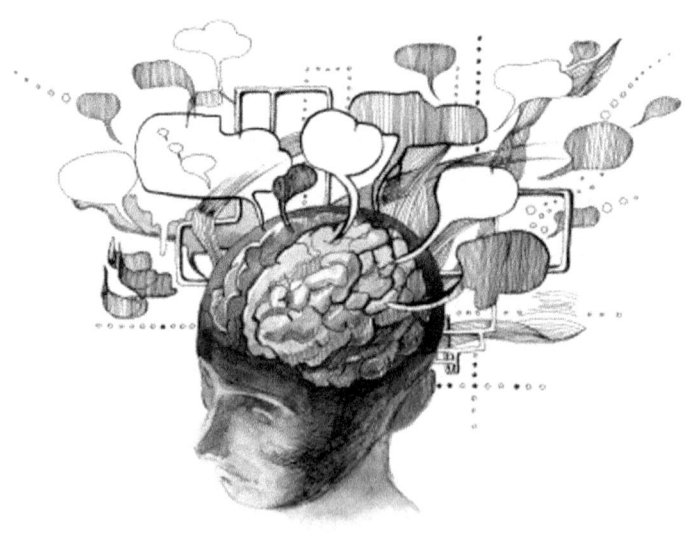

Memory

Before we get into our process for story development, let's talk briefly about long-term memory. We care about memory for two reasons: 1) we want our stories to be remembered and 2) we want to reinforce our stories in our own memories so we can retell them with confidence.

Two main factors determine what information is committed to long-term memory:

- the amount of processing done on the new information, and

- the number of mental connections which can be made between new and existing information.

Amount of Processing:

The more time and effort you spend processing new information, the more likely you are to remember it. A good example is that of taking notes in a class. When you take notes, you are more likely to remember because while you are seeing and hearing the original content, your brain is sorting the important from the trivial, you are physically writing it down, and you see what you have written. You are essentially creating multiple channels for the information to get into your brain. Processing also refers to how much you think about the new information or practice it afterwards.

By thinking about, working with, telling, and writing your professional success stories, you will reinforce the details and improve the clarity of your stories in your own mind. Structuring and then practicing your stories will reinforce how you deliver them. Don't worry; it isn't hard because you already know your stories. You have lived them. However, to draw a bit of a parallel, a good stand-up comedian knows that structure, details, practice, and timing make a big difference. The effort you put into developing your stories will have a direct effect on how well you respond to interview questions.

Mental connections:

Mental connections are the fabric of our memory. The ease with which we can build mental connections or establish something in memory depends on how similar the new information is to something we already know. If I tell you I just got a new Wassnit, you don't know what to imagine. But, when I tell you my Wassnit is bright green and has wings you begin to form a picture in your mind.

To make a story stick, we want it to be new yet related to what our audience can already understand. The more your audience can connect to your information *and imagine it,* the more likely they will engage and remember. Communicating using story increases our ability to connect.

Here is a short personal example to demonstrate:

I was on my first business trip to Lake Charles, Louisiana and decided I would like to go to the Creole Nature Trail in my spare time in hopes of seeing an alligator. Prior to my trip I had only seen alligators in a zoo and I thought it would be an experience to see one in the wild.

No one in the office wanted to go, so after work I drove about an hour by myself to the wildlife refuge. By the time I arrived it was dusk and there was absolutely no one else at the trail - no cars and no people.

I was having second thoughts. However, I'd come this far and wasn't going to have another chance on the trip; so, I went in. The trail is about 5 feet wide and rises only about 6 inches above the water level of the swamp on either side.

I walked about a mile and a half and saw nothing but blackish water and grass patches.

It was a big disappointment! Then, all of a sudden, I heard a loud rustling in the grass to my left. A six-foot alligator tore out of the grass and swam at lightning speed toward me across the water. It put half of its body onto the path about 7 feet in front of me, opened its mouth wide, and began whacking its tail back and forth on the water. I was terrified!

I saw an alligator. I don't want to see another one except in a zoo.

My guess is that you mentally joined me on my trip to the swamp and felt some of what I felt - first disappointment and then fear for my life. As humans we are programmed to put ourselves in the shoes of the character as a way to imprint our own minds for the benefit of our own self-preservation. Telling a story that elicits emotions will create deep and automatic connections with your audience because we have all felt fear, embarrassment, inspiration, joy, etc. The easiest way to build connections in your audience's mind is to tap into emotion. The more mental connections made, and the more emotionally powerful they are, the better chance your listener will engage and remember.

Conventional wisdom in the business world says we should condense information into tight bullet points, stick to the facts, and get to the point. This makes sense for efficiency's sake but not for lasting memory and creating human connection.

In an interview it is more important to connect with your interviewer than to spew facts about what you have done. With a little effort, you can turn your business results into stories that are nearly as engaging as one about a wild alligator. If you do, your interviewer will not only understand 'what' you have achieved but also get a sense of 'who' you are. They will form a human connection with you.

We Remember Stories

Now that we've talked a bit about how memory is influenced, we would like to share two quick studies that we think reinforce the point.

Chip Heath, a Stanford professor, columnist for *Fast Company*, and co-author of the book *Made to Stick*, conducted the following experiment with his students: Each student was required to give a one-minute presentation that would be rated by their classmates. Students came from a variety of backgrounds and some were not native English speakers. A few were excellent speakers, while others were nervous and awkward. Not surprisingly, students gave higher ratings to the more polished speakers.

After the initial ranking, they had the students watch a 10 minute Monty Python clip, then tested them on what they remembered from the speeches. The results were very different. It didn't matter how smoothly the information was delivered. What mattered most to retention was the form of delivery. The speeches where stories were used were remembered by significantly more students than speeches that just stated facts.

The book *Influencer* describes a different study where MBA students were divided into three groups and given the same information about a business case but in different formats. The first group was given the information in the form of facts and figures; the second, in the form of charts and graphs; and the third in the form of a story about a little old wine maker.

Several weeks later, the researchers came back and tested the students' memory of the case. The students in the third group, who were given the story, remembered more detail about the case. Additionally, the group who had been given the story found the information to be more credible than the other two groups did. In other words, they thought the case could have been real. This is an important point because if you deliver your information in story format it will not only have a better chance of being remembered, but will also have a better chance of being perceived as credible.

When you hear a story, you identify with the characters, imagine the situation happening, and experience emotions as if you were a participant. Your brain processes the information and builds connections that make for strong and retrievable memories. Most importantly, story builds human connection.

Success Stories 101 8-Step Model

Prepare		
(1)	Capture what happened	
(2)	State your point	

Structure		Beginning	Situation
(3)	Grab their attention	Beginning	Situation
(4)	Set the stage		
(5)	Describe the decisive moment	Middle	Task & Action
(6)	Depict the challenges		
(7)	Reveal the results	End	Results

Refine		
(8)	Tell your story	
	Write your story	

The 8-Step Process

A good story is one that paints a picture, evokes emotions, and lets the listener experience it. While there is not necessarily a right or wrong way to develop a story, we have created an 8-step process based on various books, research, and screen writing techniques that should help you frame a coherent and compelling story. Our model aligns with several interview response methodologies but we include a few additional steps that emphasize the human story rather than just producing a connected set of information that rushes to convey a numeric result.

At the most basic level, a story can be broken into a beginning, middle, and end. A popular method for interview response, which is taught at many MBA programs, is the STAR method (Situation, Task, Action, Results). The STAR and a number of other similar methods are for preparing a structured response to interview questions such as 'Tell me about a time when you faced a challenge.' It makes sense that an interview response should be structured. If you look at our 8-step graphic you will see how the beginning, middle, and end and the STAR methods map to our 8-steps. The models are congruent.

However, we emphasize story development and making a human connection over preparing a short answer response which focuses heavily on the technical (data) results achieved. This may seem counter-intuitive. Don't we want to get as many hard results out in an interview as we can in the time limit that we have? Not necessarily. Remember that story, more than a list of facts, sticks in memory and is perceived as credible. You will be better off if you connect with the human who is interviewing you. We will address story length in a minute; but, let's do a quick overview of the 8-step process first.

Steps 1 and 2 of the process are for preparation. It is important to take some time to refresh your own memory and capture details about your achievement before you try to structure it. Deciding up front on the main point of your story will ensure you do not wander off topic while developing it.

Steps 3 through 7 are where you will structure your story. You will start your story with a grab that quickly draws your listener in. Then you will provide enough context that they can see the bigger picture. You will describe your decisive moment and why you took action when perhaps others didn't. Next you will depict the challenges, letting your audience understand that it wasn't easy. Finally, you will close by sharing the results and by making the main point which you established in Step 2.

In step 8 you will refine your story: first by telling it, then by writing it. We emphasize telling your story in order to keep it conversational in style and tone. We want it to be inviting. Inevitably, developing your story the first time will most likely not yield a perfect result. Improving your story is an iterative editing process. During the editing process you can begin to address the length of your story as appropriate. Once you have a good first pass at your story, you can generally make it better by editing and tightening it.

A Note About Story Length:

In our in-person workshops we always get the question: How long should my story be? There is advice out there that interview responses should always be less than two minutes. Candidates are afraid that their stories will be too long.

Our belief is that an interview should be a conversation, not a tennis match where the interviewer lobs a question, you respond, they lob the next, you respond, and so forth.

Your goal in an interview is to make a connection with the interviewer and to talk to them about how you can add value at their company. As in any conversation, you need to read your interviewer to determine their interest level; but, if your story is engaging most people will be interested and will want to know how it turns out. Most importantly, they will remember it and believe it.

One of our workshop participants had a great answer for the question about story length. She said it was the same advice her mother gave her about the right length for a woman's skirt:

Long enough to cover what's important, but short enough to maintain interest.

Length will also vary based on the complexity of the story. Collapsing a complex story just to achieve a strict time limit will most likely weaken it.

Part of the value of developing your stories using the 8-step process is to structure and to clarify them in your own mind. Then, when you tell your stories you will not struggle to remember details or go off on tangents, losing your train of thought, and wasting time. You will be able to tell a compelling and memorable story that makes a clear point in an appropriate amount of time.

During your first pass through the 8-step process we don't want you to worry about length. The primary goal at this stage is to get the story captured and structured. You will go back later to edit, refine, and compact as appropriate.

At this point, choose an accomplishment you would like to develop into a story while going through our 8-step process.

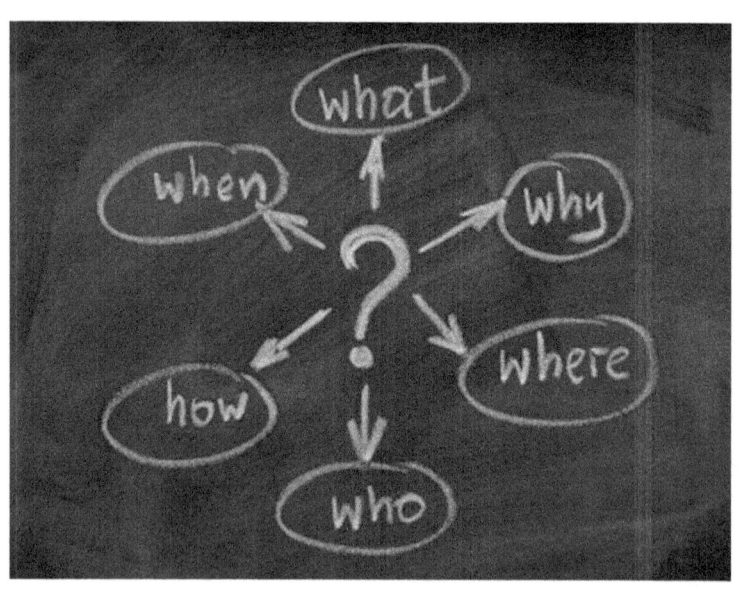

Step 1: Capture what happened

Great stories draw us in through the use of vivid details and emotional connections. Before you can paint a picture in the minds of your audience, you need to remember it yourself.

Take a few minutes to mentally put yourself back into the situation. In addition to the statistical and factual details of the circumstances, try to capture the emotional essence of the incident for you and the others that were involved. Facts, details, and business results are important; but, wrapping them in the feeling of the situation will help your listener connect and be empathetic.

This step is just for remembering and jotting down notes about what happened. Do not try to write a story yet. Don't edit and don't worry about whether your notes are usable or relevant. The idea is to stimulate thought and memories. As you jot one note down, another memory will break free.

Try to "see" what it looked like, "hear" what it sounded like, and "feel" what it felt like. Was it a tense situation? Were people angry? Was there fear, joy, confusion, frustration, emergency?

Take about 5 minutes on Step 1.

_____

_____

_____

_____

_____

_____

_____

_____

_____

_____

_____

_____

_____

_____

_____

_____

_____

_____

_____

_____

_____

_____

_____

_____

_____

_____

_____

_____

_____

_____

Step 2: State your point

Now that you've had some time to reflect on your situation, you need to decide upfront what your main point is going to be.

While your story is about something you experienced, you need to keep in mind that you are telling the story for the benefit of your listener. Why are you telling this story? What do you expect your interviewer to remember?

Try to resist the idea that the point of your story must be the same as the end business result, say a 10% increase in profit. You will definitely want to include this data in your story but it may not be your main point.

As an illustration, if you climbed to the top of Mt. Everest, your point would not necessarily be that you reached the top, but rather that you possess the determination, drive, and perseverance to have taken the journey.

Another thing to consider is that it is rare that the hiring company will have exactly the same problem you solved already; but, they probably will have the need for the skills, problem solving, leadership, etc. that you used in your achievement. Your main point should emphasize your transferable skills while the data (X% improvement in Y) will be used to support your point.

Obviously, the interviewer wants to see that you have delivered results. However, if he or she gets to see your character as well, they will be more likely to want you on their team.

The most powerful story will be *about* something you accomplished but that *highlights your strengths and your potential for future accomplishments.*

Take a few minutes to write down the main point of your story. Here are a few things to ask yourself:

1. What is the one idea I want my interviewer to walk away with?

2. What conclusion do I expect the listener to reach?

3. How would I answer if my interviewer asked, "So What?"

_____
_____
_____
_____
_____
_____
_____
_____
_____
_____
_____

Step 3: Grab their attention

The best stories start off with a strong "hook". The first line of a novel is often funny, unusual, or unexpected. It is designed to create interest and to make the reader want to keep reading.

The key to grabbing and holding your audience's attention is to create questions in their minds and to make them wonder what is going to happen next.

In 1994, George Loewenstein, a behavioral economist at Carnegie Mellon University, proposed the "gap theory" of curiosity. He says that curiosity happens when we sense a gap in our knowledge. He suggests that when we want to know something but don't, it is like having an itch we need to scratch. We feel compelled to "fill" our mental gaps.

Try to begin your story in a way that arouses curiosity and makes the listener want to know more.

Here's one of my stories:

I was recruited for a new position by a colleague whom I had worked with while I was a management consultant several years earlier. The job was on the other side of the country; but, it was close to my wife's family so we welcomed a move.

I accepted the position, quit my job at the bank, and flew across the country to begin my new job.

On my first day, my new boss asked me to meet him outside the building so we could go to lunch from there. When I met him, the first words out of his mouth were, "I have some bad news."

Are you curious about what happened next?

Here are a few other first-line examples that came up in our workshops:

The project was over budget and three months behind schedule. Morale was at an all-time low. That is when I got roped in.

There was nothing in my job description about taking care of a rat infestation in the parking lot.

Every morning two security guards would meet me in the parking lot, for my own protection, to escort me into the building to my desk.

The Federal Reserve has a lot of secrets...

Take a few minutes to create a grab that will make your listener want to know more.

_____

_____

_____

_____

_____

_____

_____

Step 4: Set the stage

As you begin your story, you will need to provide your audience with enough context to understand the scope of the situation before you jump into what you did or how you made things better. Your "grab" may start to do this; but, this step is where you need to make sure your audience can visualize the problem and put themselves into your shoes.

Include relevant details that will add credibility to your story. Look back at your notes from Step 1 where you captured what you saw, felt, heard, etc.

When setting up the problem, *make it personal.* People respond to human problems – things they can relate to. Show the audience what was at stake for the people involved. Describe the risks of action or of inaction. If your audience senses the danger or significance of the situation, you help them connect emotionally. They will care about what happens and will want to know how the story ends.

This is the point where you may want to introduce some numbers or statistics to frame the problem; so, we want to provide some tips. Keep numbers and statistics on a 'human scale' or use an analogy to help your audience relate to the values.

If I say we increased output by 7,981,240 units, what does that mean? It could be a lot or it could be nothing relative to overall production levels. Additionally, most people have a hard time visualizing large numbers. Percentages have a similar problem. If I say we increased sales by 5%, is that a big deal or is it trivial? We need context to understand the significance of the values.

Here is a real example of what we mean:

In 2009 the Susan G. Komen Foundation put out the following breast cancer awareness ad:

It is estimated that in 2009,

192,370 new breast cancer cases are expected to be found in females in the United States. This year,

40,170 women will lose their battle with breast cancer.

192,370 is a big number and 40,170 is a lot of women; but, what does it really mean to you? Are you relating to and connecting with the information?

Now read the billboard campaign they ran in October of 2010 and contrast how it affects you:

Think of 8 women you know.

Now, pick one.

1 in 8 women are diagnosed with breast cancer in their lifetime.

In the 2010 example, the meaning of the statistics suddenly becomes crystal clear because it is in a context we can relate to. These numbers are on a 'human scale.' It is hard to imagine 192,370 women, and you would probably have to look up the page to even remember the number. But is easy to imagine 8 women we know. This example packs an emotional punch you are unlikely to forget.

Another way of dealing with complex values is to use an analogy. In his book <u>The 8th Habit</u>, Steven Covey describes the results of an employee poll where only 37% of employees had a clear understanding of what their organization was trying to achieve and why. Covey used the following analogy: "If, say, a soccer team had these same scores, only 4 of the 11 players on the field would know which goal is theirs. Only 2 of the 11 would care." The analogy has more impact than the percentage because we can imagine it, relate to it, and visualize just how pathetic the situation was.

If your statistics are easy enough for people to understand there is no need to get too creative. But, you need to ask yourself whether your numbers are on a human scale and help convey the true magnitude of the situation.

Please note that whereas we have spent a disproportionate amount of time providing tips for this step, it does not mean that this step should be lengthy. You are simply trying to provide some context. Use relevant details and numbers that support your main point (step 2) and try to minimize distractions or going off on tangents.

Take a few minutes to "set the stage" for your story by asking yourself:

1. What details are required to establish the context of my story?

2. What information do I need to provide to help them understand the problem?

3. How can I describe the problem in a way that makes it personal? (on a human scale?)

4. How can I show the audience what was at stake?

_____

_____

_____

_____

_____

_____

_____

_____

_____

_____

_____

_____

_____

_____

_____

_____

_____

_____

_____

_____

_____

_____

_____

_____

_____

_____

_____

_____

_____

_____

_____

_____

_____

Step 5: Describe the decisive moment

There is a turning point in every story where the hero makes the fateful decision to act. You are the hero of your story. You may have decided to face a fear, take a risk, or stand up for something important.

Describe what motivated, drove, or inspired you to act. Explain your thought process. Show how you devised the solution or took charge of the situation. This is a key step that will help your listener connect to you and your story. Letting someone inside your head enables them to understand why you did what you did and gives them a sense of who you are as a person.

While we were writing this book, we heard a good example of a decisive moment in a story on NPR's Morning Edition. Host Steve Inskeep was talking about Mitt Romney during the January 2012 Republican primary. Here is a transcript clip:

> STEVE INSKEEP... Though it's common to say that Mitt Romney has been seeking the presidency for years, Ann Romney contends there was a moment, one year ago, when he almost decided not to run.
>
> ANN ROMNEY: And we knew there would be challengers and there would be issues and there would be problems. And then if you even got the nomination, we knew how difficult it is, but I asked him one question, and this is why we decided to run. I said, Mitt, can you save America? And his answer was Yes. ..."

Regardless of your political preference, hearing this story about a presidential candidate's decisive moment says something about him as a person. You can tell there was contemplation. There is a relationship of trust and encouragement with his wife. And finally, a motivational belief (albeit lofty).

Your decision or turning point is what thrusts your story into motion. Up until now you have gotten your listener's attention and set up the problem. This step shows how you decided to tackle it head on.

Ask yourself:

1. What made you choose to act when others did not?

2. What motivated you or who inspired you?

3. How did you come up with the solution?

4. What was your thought process?

Step 6: Depict the challenges

This part of your story is about the journey and what happened along the way. Most significant achievements don't come with just a single hurdle. Things almost never go exactly as planned.

Many of us have a tendency, especially in an interview, to play down the difficulties we faced in order to make it sound like everything was easy for us. We want people to think we are smart and that challenges are a snap for us. But, this can be a mistake because it may minimize the true magnitude of the achievement.

Have you ever watched an athlete stumble at the start of the race, then pick himself up, keep going, and somehow manage to come back to win? How much more impressive is it than if he had never fallen?

Your ability to overcome obstacles is part of your value. Acknowledging a false start or admitting you were terrified and didn't know what to do is alright because you are going to go on to tell how you resolved the challenge. The stark contrast will make the story more compelling and more credible - and your results will appear as impressive as they ought to be. Additionally, as each challenge unfolds it creates new information gaps, keeping your listener wanting to know what happens next.

Robert McKee, a famous screenwriting coach, puts it this way, "A good story is not the beginning-to-end tale about how results met expectations. This is boring. Avoid this. Instead it's better to illustrate the **struggle** between expectation and reality ..."

One quick word of caution for this step is that you should be careful not to come across as being negative in the way you describe your challenges. You can describe the contrast of the situation without using a negative tone.

Take a few minutes to capture the challenges you faced and how you overcame them.

1. What were the challenges?
2. How did you respond?
3. How can you keep the listeners wondering what is going to happen next?

_____

_____

_____

_____

_____

_____

_____

_____

_____

_____

_____

_____

_____

_____

_____

_____

_____

_____

_____

_____

_____

_____

_____

_____

_____

Step 7: Reveal the results

The last part of your story should provide resolution and make your point (revisit Step 2).

Try to show how things were better for the people involved at the end of the journey. Use numeric results such as a 15% increase in profit to support your achievement; but, you want a conclusion with a human story. Think of it this way. You want your listener to feel like you felt when you succeeded.

Compare and contrast the following variations of the same achievement:

A) My process innovation made the sales people, who initially resisted the change, happy because their deals went through three times faster than before. They felt more in control, and they had the potential to do more deals and make more money for themselves and the company.

B) My project resulted in a 300% improvement in deal velocity and increased revenue.

Which do you think is better? Why?

Most advice I have seen on STAR and other methods places emphasis on the statistical result (version B) because there is a misconception that statistics are what make the result credible. However, as we discussed in the beginning of the book, story with human connection trumps raw data.

Option A, in contrast, provides the results in human terms. We can see how people's lives were made better by the new process and can imagine the benefits for them and for the company. An interviewer might think "I would like John on our team because he can make the Sales guys happy." Keep in mind the achievement is the same; it is simply the form of delivery that is different.

You may start out with something that looks like version B; but, we encourage you to look a bit deeper to see if there is a human triumph, however small, that can help your listener feel like you and others did when you succeeded.

A few of our workshop participants have asked: What if my story didn't turn out positively? For example, the company went bankrupt. Even in such a case, there can be hidden success stories about how you or others were somehow changed for the better by the event or learned something from it.

Help your audience see how you can take your experience and apply it to other challenges.

Take a few minutes to craft the resolution to your story.

- How did it all turn out?
- How were things different afterwards?
- How were things better for the people involved?
- How did you grow from the experience?

- What did you learn from the experience?
- Are there any measurable results?

_____

_____

_____

_____

_____

_____

_____

_____

_____

_____

_____

_____

_____

_____

_____

_____

_____

_____

_____

_____

_____

_____

_____

_____

_____

_____

_____

_____

_____

_____

Step 8a: Tell your story

At this point in our workshop, we pair up participants and have them tell their stories to each other. Telling your story to a friend is an important step because you want to work out the kinks and learn to deliver your story in a conversational way.

Here are some steps to follow to get ready to tell your story the first time:

- Read what you wrote from Steps 3 to Step 7 (your story).

- Make sure your story flows across the steps and that you ultimately make your main point (Go back and review Step 2).

- Adjust and tweak as needed.

- Now you are ready to tell your story to a friend.

Telling your story is a great way to check for the following:

- Your story is clear, flows well, and avoids going off on tangents.

- Your story is conversational and inviting, free of corporate babble (acronyms and jargon) that turns people off and might not be understood.

- Your story maintains interest and curiosity.

- Your story makes your point.

Step 8b: Write/Revise your story

Once you have told your story and received feedback, we recommend you revise it in writing. Editing it in writing reinforces the story in your mind and you will have a record to review later, perhaps before each interview.

After your have revised your story you may want to iterate the cycle of telling and revising until you are satisfied. It's a good idea to put your story away for a day or two between cycles and return to it with fresh eyes and perspective. Finally, watch for places to cut. We almost always write too much at first.

Remember that you want to have a story that is long enough to cover what is important but short enough to be interesting. Edit, rewrite, refine.

The more you work with your story by practicing telling it and working with the written version, the more you will reinforce it in your mind. When you are asked in an interview to "Tell me about a time when...", you will be able to share your story with confidence and make your point in a clear, compelling, and memorable way.

Below is a checklist to consider while reviewing your story:

- Started with a grab to draw people in and to make them want to know the outcome.
- Provided enough context for non-experts to engage in and understand the story.
- Described the decisive moment and let people see your thought process.

- Used enough relevant details for credibility, but kept the story short enough to have impact.
- Created a natural flow in the story that maintains interest and led to the main point.
- Described what was going on with the people involved, made it a human story that people can connect with.
- Made your main point.

Note: The story you have written should be *used as a guide* when you tell the story in an interview. The idea is not to recite your story as you have written it, but to know the structure and flow of your story well enough to tell it with confidence.

We hope you have enjoyed this course and we hope using our 8-step process enables you to more confidently demonstrate your value in interviews. Good luck!

Notes:

Memory

Pages 13-18: There is a detailed discussion of the factors that affect what gets added to our long term memory on pages 350-356 of: Lindsay, Peter H., Donald A. Norman. <u>Human Information Processing, An Introduction to Psychology</u>. Second Edition. New York: Academic Press, Inc. 1977.

We Remember Stories

Pages 21-22: The story of the Stanford class experiment can be found on page 242 of: Heath, Chip, and Dan Heath. <u>Made to Stick: Why Some Ideas Survive and Others Die</u>. New York: Random House, 2008. This was a terrific book and well worth a full read. Some of the other ideas we've touched on in this workshop are also covered in more detail in *Made to Stick*.

Pages 22-23: The story of the MBA students who were given the same business case in different formats begins on page 60 of: Patterson, Kerry, et al. <u>Influencer: the Power to Change Anything</u>. New York: McGraw-Hill, 2008.

The 8 Step Process

Our 8 steps were created based on universal storytelling principles found in many books we've read over the years but we want to acknowledge the excellent discussion of plot structure in Chapter 2 of: Bell, James Scott. <u>Write Great Fiction: Plot & Structure: techniques and exercises for crafting a plot that grips readers from start to finish</u>. Cincinnati: Writer's Digest Books. 2004.

Step 3, Grab Their Attention

Page 43-44: Professor Lowenstien's theory of curiosity can be found in: Loewenstein, George. "The Psychology of Curiosity: A Review and Reinterpretation." <u>Psychological Bulletin</u> 1994: Vol. 116. No.1. 75-98.

Step 4, Set the Stage

Pages 52: The results of the Harris poll and the soccer team analogy that illustrates it are found on pages 2-3 of the book: Covey, Steven. The 8th Habit From Effectiveness to Greatness. New York: Free Press, 2005.

Step 5, Describe the Decisive Moment

Page 58: Transcript clip of interview with Mitt and Ann Romney was from: Inskeep, Steve. "Romney Maintains The Style Of A Front-Runner" Morning Edition. National Public Radio. WFAE, Charlotte NC. 10 January 2012.

Step 6, Depict the Challenges

Page 62: McKee, Robert , Bronwyn Fryer. "Storytelling That Moves People, " Harvard Business Review. Jun 01, 2003 4 pages.

When executives need to persuade an audience, most try to build a case with facts, statistics, and some quotes from authorities. In other words, they resort to "companyspeak," the tools of rhetoric they have been trained to use.

In this conversation with HBR, Robert McKee, the world's best-known screenwriting lecturer, argues that executives can engage people in a much deeper--and ultimately more convincing--way if they toss out their PowerPoint slides and memos and learn to tell good stories.

Additional Resources:

Books and Articles:

Gruber, Peter. "Four Truths of the Storyteller." <u>Harvard Business Review</u>. Dec 01, 2007. 9 pages.

A well-told story's power to captivate and inspire people has been recognized for thousands of years. Peter Gruber is in the business of creating compelling stories: He has headed several entertainment companies--including Sony Pictures, PolyGram, and Columbia Pictures--and produced Rain Man, Batman, and The Color Purple, among many other movies. In this article, he offers a method for effectively exercising that power.

Klaus, Peggy. <u>Brag! The Art of Tooting Your Own Horn Without Blowing It</u>. New York: Hachette Book Group, 2003.

McKee, Robert. <u>Story: Substance, Structure, Style and the Principles of Screenwriting</u>. New York: Regan, 1997.

Simmons, Annette. <u>The Story Factor: Secrets of Influence from the Art of Storytelling.</u> New York: Basic, 2006.

Web Resources:

www.intRvue.com is our web application where you can share your success stories online in multimedia. Get **3 months of intRvue FREE** with coupon code: **hbk213tni.**

Ira Glass on Storytelling- Four part series available on YouTube offers great advice from the host of <u>This American Life.</u>

Making You Stick – free podcast from Dan Heath available at **http://heathbrothers.com/resources/**

Success Stories 101 Online:

By purchasing this book and for no additional cost, you can access our online workshop that includes training videos and space to develop and store your stories on our web application. You can also print additional 8-step worksheets if you prefer to work on paper.

To create your FREE account, go to www.successstories101.com and use access code **8ss-101-int**. You will also need to enter your Amazon, Create Space, or other receipt/order number.

If you have any trouble signing in please contact us.

Contact Us

We are interested in your feedback and we would especially like to hear about your success in sharing stories that you developed and refined using our process!

If you have a group or school that you think would benefit from Success Stories 101, please call us for group discounts on our e-book and online service.

If you have a group that would benefit from an in-person workshop, please contact us for rates and availability.

Email us at Sales@intRvue.com or call at (704) 483-1950